BARBARA JOHNSON

Every Time I Get My Act Together, the Curtain Comes Down!

Every Time I Get My Act Together,
The Curtain Comes Down

Copyright © 1995, Barbara Johnson
Published by Garborg's Heart 'n Home, Inc.
P.O. Box 20132
Bloomington, MN 55420

SPCN 5-5044-0287-5

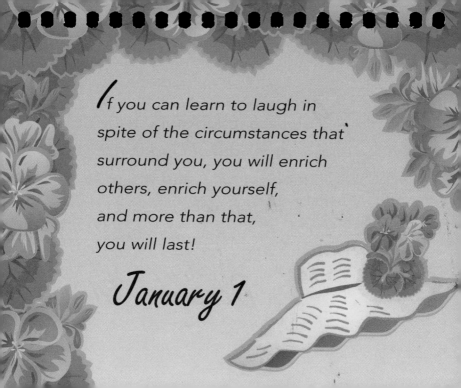

If you can learn to laugh in
spite of the circumstances that
surround you, you will enrich
others, enrich yourself,
and more than that,
you will last!

January 1

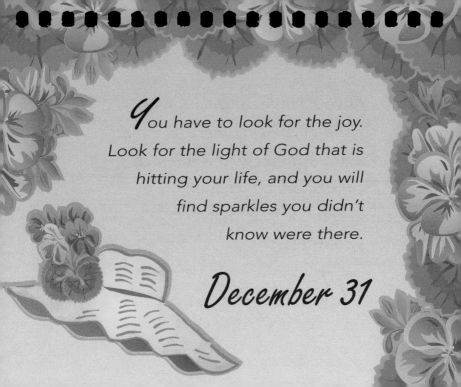

You have to look for the joy. Look for the light of God that is hitting your life, and you will find sparkles you didn't know were there.

December 31

I always feel good about the start of a new year. To many of us, January is the eraser God provides to wipe the slate clean.

January 2

If in the last year you haven't discarded a major opinion or acquired a new one, check your pulse—you may be dead!

December 30

*B*umper sticker for hypochondriacs: "I'd rather be ailing."

January 3

*A*t day's end, I turn all my problems over to God....
He's going to be up anyway.

December 29

Too many people think that a thought a day means having just one thought a day.

January 4

God will accept a broken heart, but He must have all the pieces.

December 28

*T*here was a young gal from
    Montana,
who did not see the banana.
She skidded ten feet
and the sidewalk did meet,
and now she can't play
    the piana.

January 5

*L*ife is a great big canvas,
and you should throw all the
paint on it you can.

December 27

What this country needs is another holiday—a day set aside to celebrate having survived all the others.

January 6

*R*emember, the Christmas presents of today are the garage sales of tomorrow.

December 26

It's a proven fact that working out will increase your bust size. Unfortunately, it will also give you a neck the size of a Quaker Oats box.

January 7

Bethlehem's stable was the first step in God's love-journey to Calvary's cross.

December 25

I am better than I was, but not quite so good as I was before I got worse.

January 8

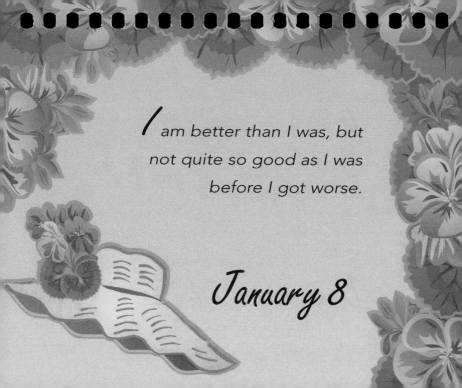

*W*hen you stop believing in Santa Claus, you get underwear for Christmas.

December 24

The secret to dealing successfully with a child is to not be its parent.

January 9

Christmas Love: He came to pay a debt He didn't owe because we owed a debt we couldn't pay.

December 23

A good friend puts up with your worst moods, goes along with your worst ideas, and always sees the best in you.

January 10

Man is born broken; he lives by mending. The grace of God is the glue.

December 22

*A*musing grace...how sweet the sound of laughter.

January 11

*E*ncouragement is like
premium gas. It helps to take
the knocks out of living.

December 21

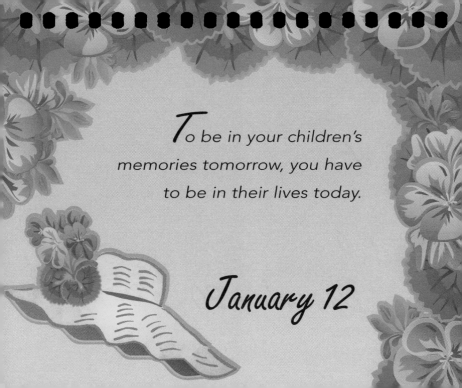

To be in your children's memories tomorrow, you have to be in their lives today.

January 12

*F*amilies are like fudge...
mostly sweet, with a few nuts.

December 20

The blue of heaven is bigger
than the clouds.

January 13

Godliness is the ability to let your light shine after your fuse is blown.

December 19

*W*ho supplies another
with a constructive thought
has enriched him forever.

January 14

*F*aith is seeing light with your heart, when all your eyes see is the darkness ahead.

December 18

A smile is the lighting system of the face and the heating system of the heart.

January 15

*J*oy is not the absence of
suffering, but the
presence of God.

December 17

There's nothing wrong with having nothing to say, as long as you don't say it out loud.

January 16

In my father's house are many mansions.... I hope yours is next to mine!

December 16

*T*he handwriting on the wall means that the grandchildren have found the crayons.

January 17

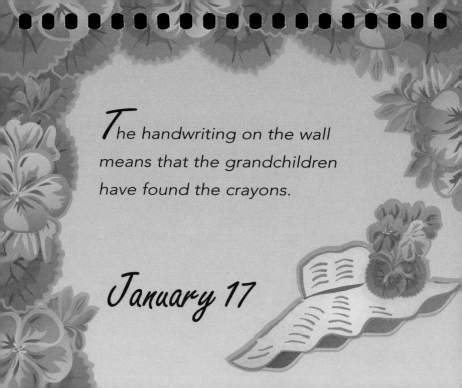

*T*hose proud of keeping an orderly desk never know the thrill of finding something they thought they had irretrievably lost.

December 15

God calls us to be faithful;
He did not promise we
would be successful.

January 18

It's not the mountain that wears you out—it's the grain of sand in your shoe.

December 14

*W*hen the going gets tough...
we gotta be tougher!

January 19

*N*othing is as hard to do
gracefully as getting down
off your high horse.

December 13

A friend is one who strengthens you with prayers, blesses you with love, and encourages you with hope.

January 20

*E*njoy today...God loves to hear
your laughter.

December 12

*F*aith doesn't panic.

January 21

I'm glad God has all the answers, 'cause I barely understand the questions.

December 11

Middle age is when you choose your cereal for the fiber, not the toy.

January 22

Laughter is a tranquilizer with no side effects.

December 10

*T*he end is not near...
you must learn to cope.

January 23

*P*rogress always involves risks.
You can't steal second base and
keep your foot on first.

December 9

*T*he smartest advice on raising
children is to enjoy them while
they are still on your side.

January 24

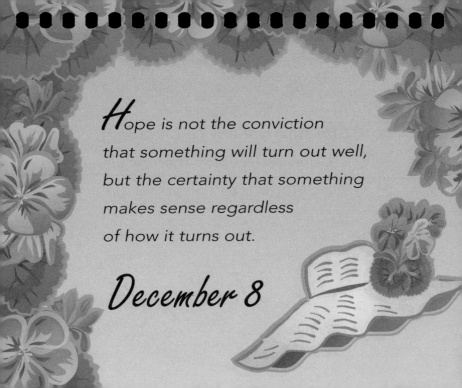

Hope is not the conviction that something will turn out well, but the certainty that something makes sense regardless of how it turns out.

December 8

It's not the load that brings you down, it's the way you carry it.

January 25

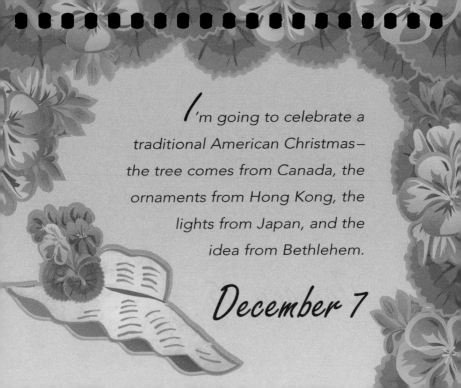

I'm going to celebrate a traditional American Christmas—the tree comes from Canada, the ornaments from Hong Kong, the lights from Japan, and the idea from Bethlehem.

December 7

Frogs have it easy; they can
eat what bugs them.

January 26

*A*dvice is like snow; the softer it falls, the deeper it sinks.

December 6

*S*houting to make your children obey is like using the horn to steer your car, and you get about the same results.

January 27

*P*resence makes a happy family.

December 5

A keen sense of humor helps us to overlook the unbecoming, understand the unconventional, tolerate the unpleasant, overcome the unexpected, and outlast the unbearable.

January 28

*A*ll that is worth cherishing in
this world begins in the heart,
not in the head.

December 4

If you talk too much you'll probably say too much.

January 29

*L*aughter is the sun that drives
winter from one's face.

December 3

A lot of people get through thinking before they get through thinking things through.

January 30

*P*ack up your "gloomees"
in a great big box,
then sit on the lid
and laugh!

December 2

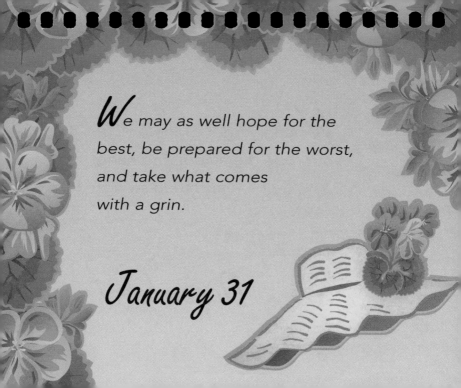

*W*e may as well hope for the best, be prepared for the worst, and take what comes with a grin.

January 31

*W*hen you get to the end of
your rope, tie a knot and hang
on—and then swing!

December 1

*W*hen you're down and out,
lift up you head and shout...
"I'm down and out!"

February 1

Confidence is what you have when you don't really understand the situation.

November 30

*O*nly some of us learn by other people's mistakes; the rest of us have to be the other people.

February 2

Life is an endless struggle,
full of frustrations and challenges,
but eventually you find a
hairstylist you like!

November 29

If you're headed in the wrong direction, God allows U-turns.

February 3

Laughing helps.

It's like jogging on the inside.

November 28

*T*he three grand essentials
of happiness are something
to do, someone to love, and
something to hope for.

February 4

Keep sending out love messages. Even if you feel you are trying to hug a porcupine, keep sharing your heart!

November 27

You feel right when
you do right.

February 5

Today's mighty oak is just yeterday's nut that held its ground.

November 26

If it's free, it's advice;
if you pay for it, it's counseling;
if you can use either one,
it's a miracle!

February 6

*P*ractical guide for successful living: Put your head under the pillow and scream.

November 25

*M*an cannot live by bread alone;
he needs peanut butter.

February 7

*L*et your arithmetic be at its best
when counting blessings.

November 24

*A*n old-timer is anyone
who learned to ride a bicycle
before it became a
fitness machine.

February 8

*D*on't worry about the world
ending today. I'ts already
tomorrow in Australia.

November 23

*A*dmit your errors before
someone else exaggerates them.

February 9

*T*he weather may be abominable,
the skies may be cloudy and murky,
but everybody will have a good time...
everybody, that is, but the turkey.

November 22

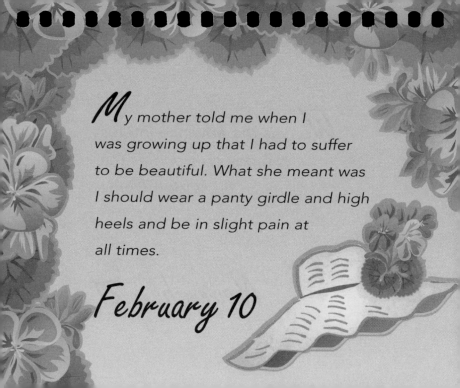

*M*y mother told me when I was growing up that I had to suffer to be beautiful. What she meant was I should wear a panty girdle and high heels and be in slight pain at all times.

February 10

*Worry is the advance interest
you pay on troubles that
seldom come.*

November 21

*L*ove sees through a telescope,
not a microscope.

February 11

You are a child of God—
call home.

November 20

*Y*ou who have endured the stinging experiences are the choicest counselors God can use.

February 12

*C*hoice, not chance,
determines destiny.

November 19

What you do with Christ here will determine what He will do with you in the hereafter.

February 13

*T*hank You, dear God,

for all that You have given me,

for all You have taken from me,

for all You have left me!

November 18

*T*alking is sharing,
but listening is caring.

February 14

Something to be thankful for is that you're here to be thankful.

November 17

*R*eason to smile: Every seven minutes of every day, someone in an aerobics class pulls a hamstring.

February 15

Perhaps you have heard
of the little boy who prayed,
"Father, forgive us our trespasses,
as we give it to those who
trespass against us."

November 16

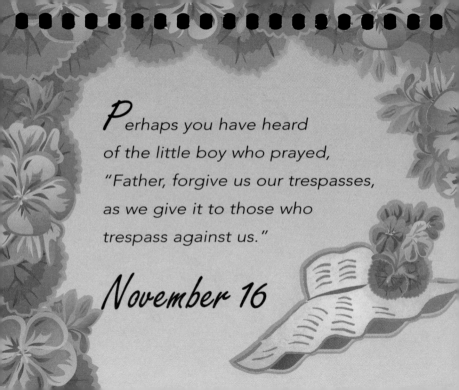

*F*aith can move mountains,
but only hard work can put a
tunnel through them.

February 16

*T*he patient conceal impatience.

November 15

It's not easy being perfect, but somebody has to do it!

February 17

*T*he most difficult meal for the average housewife to get is— dinner out!

November 14

*T*here is a chord in every heart
that has a sigh in it if you use
the right touch.

February 18

*W*isdom is the reward you get
for a lifetime of listening when
you'd have preferred to talk.

November 13

*E*very day is a free gift
from God.

February 19

Kids are like sponges: They absorb all your strength and leave you limp. But give 'em a squeeze and you get it all back.

November 12

One of my favorite
occupants of my Joy Room is
a little lady in a basket with a sign
that says, "Don't pick on me. I'm
a basket case already."

February 20

*B*lessed are the flexible, for
they shall not be bent
out of shape.

November 11

*T*he only joy some people
get out of the truth is
stretching it.

February 21

I don't mind the rat race,
but I could do with a little
more cheese.

November 10

*T*he next time you're feeling down, think about all the terrible things that didn't happen to you.

February 22

*T*here is no place for a mother
to go to resign.

November 9

A well-informed person is somebody who has the same views and opinions as yours.

February 23

*L*ife is like an ice-cream cone: Just when you think you've got it licked, it drips all over you!

November 8

*L*ord, help me to be
the kind of friend
who makes my friends secure,
that they may find
new grace and strength, their
trials to endure.

February 24

Grief is the healing mechanism
God uses, particularly when
we allow Him to enter
into the process.

November 7

*W*hen someone says,
"Life is hard," ask them,
"Compared to what?"

February 25

I hate to see you frown.
So wear a bag on your head
until you cheer up.

November 6

All we need is an ear to listen, an eye to behold, and a heart to feel.

February 26

My idea of exercise is buying a Bobby Darin record and helping him snap fingers.

November 5

The best way to keep kids at home is to make the home a pleasant atmosphere...and to let the air out of the tires.

DOROTHY PARKER

February 27

Remember when you worried because you didn't know where your children were? Now you do. They're back in their old rooms.

November 4

*L*oneliness isn't such a bad thing, except when you don't have anyone to share it with.

February 28

God said it, I believe it, and that settles it. (Then why doesn't it make any sense?)

November 3

*C*ar sickness is the feeling you get when the monthly installments come due.

February 29

Impatience: Waiting in a hurry.

November 2

*T*he real art of conversation is
not only to say the right thing in
the right place, but to leave
unsaid the wrong thing at
the tempting moment.

March 1

*W*e always have the option
to choose joy!

November 1

The secret to happiness is to count your blessings, not your birthdays.

March 2

I know that there's a thin person inside me screaming to get out. Unfortunately, she has trouble being heard through all this fat!

October 31

*R*aising a teenager is like nailing Jell-O to a tree.

March 3

*O*ne day I'll look back on
all this and laugh.

October 30

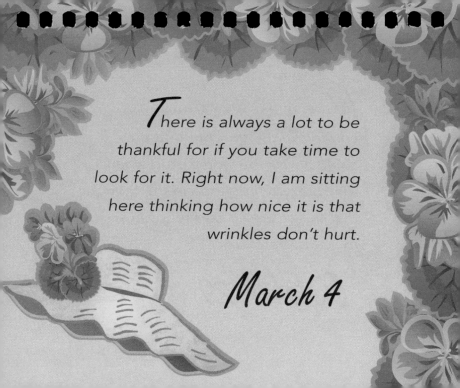

*T*here is always a lot to be thankful for if you take time to look for it. Right now, I am sitting here thinking how nice it is that wrinkles don't hurt.

March 4

*W*hen things are bad, we take comfort in the thought that they could always be worse. And when they are, we find hope in the thought that things are so bad they have to get better.

October 29

*F*aith makes the uplook good,
the outlook bright,
the inlook favorable,
and the future glorious.

March 5

*W*e tangle up the plans the Lord hath wrought, and when we cry in pain, He says, "Be quiet, dear, while I untie the knot."

October 28

God can use reverses
to move us forward.

March 6

*B*etter to better thyself...than the other fellow.

October 27

*T*he most frustrating thing in the world is when the key to success doesn't fit your ignition.

March 7

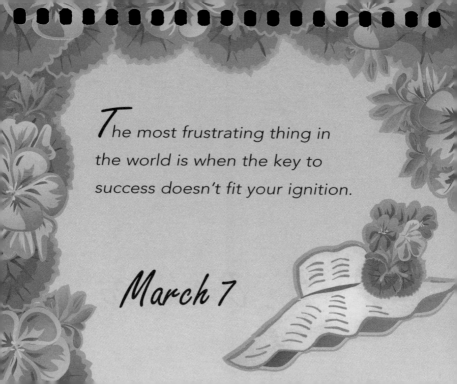

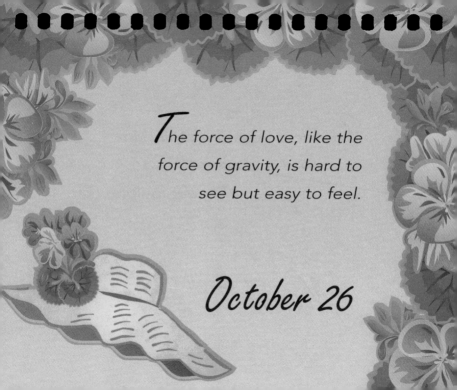

*T*he force of love, like the force of gravity, is hard to see but easy to feel.

October 26

*N*o matter how long you nurse a grudge, it won't get better.

March 8

*E*ven though I'm taking things "one day at a time," it's about twenty-four hours more than I can take.

October 25

*Q*uestion: What do you get when you cross an insomniac, an agnostic, and a dyslexic?

Answer: A person who lies awake at night trying to decide if there really is a doG.

March 9

Some people, no matter how old they get, never lose their beauty. They merely move it from their faces to their hearts.

October 24

Prayer is kind of like calling home every day.

March 10

It doesn't take monumental feats to make the world a better place. It can be as simple as letting someone go ahead of you in a grocery line.

October 23

If we give someone a piece of bread and butter, that's kindness, but if we put jelly or peanut butter on it, then it's Loving Kindness.

March 11

According to the latest
figures, if you retired today, you
could live very, very comfortably
until about 2 p.m. tomorrow.

October 22

*H*umility is like underwear—
essential, but indecent
if it shows.

March 12

Our only glory is not in never falling, but in rising each time we fall.

October 21

*P*ray for a good harvest,
but keep on hoeing.

March 13

*T*act is the rare ability to keep silent while two friends argue, all the while knowing they are both wrong.

October 20

*T*he events of our lives, when
we let God use them, become
the mysterious preparation for
the work He has prepared
us to do.

March 14

*A*s long as there are tests...
there will be prayer
in schools.

October 19

A sense of humor is like a
needle and thread: it will
patch up so many things.

March 15

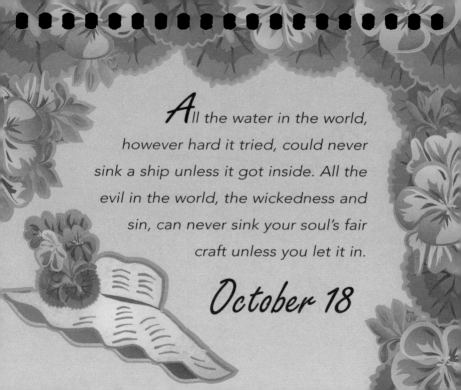

*A*ll the water in the world, however hard it tried, could never sink a ship unless it got inside. All the evil in the world, the wickedness and sin, can never sink your soul's fair craft unless you let it in.

October 18

*Silence is often misinterpreted,
but never misquoted.*

March 16

Jesus did not come to explain away suffering or remove it. He came to fill it with His presence.

October 17

*M*en have three basic hair styles: parted, unparted, and departed.

March 17

*E*ven if it burns a little low
at times, the secret of life is
to always keep the flame
of hope alive.

October 16

Insanity is my only means of relaxation.

March 18

Just when a woman thinks her work is done, she becomes a grandmother.

October 15

Life is not a matter of holding good cards. It's playing a poor hand well.

March 19

You should enjoy today while it's here, because someday today will be a long time ago.

October 14

*W*hen your dreams turn
to dust...vacuum!

March 20

Quote in a church bulletin:
The Lord loveth a cheerful giver;
He also accepteth from a grouch.

October 13

Gratitude takes three forms: a feeling in the heart, an expression in words, and giving in return.

March 21

There is no magic escape when we face insurmountable problems. We often must learn to live with mountains that will not move.

October 12

*Y*ou can't turn back the clock,
but you can wind it up again.

March 22

*P*lease Lord, teach us to laugh again, but God, don't let us forget that we cried.

October 11

*L*aughter is like changing a baby's diaper—it doesn't permanently solve any problems, but it makes things more acceptable for a while.

March 23

You may not know all the
answers, but you probably
won't be asked all the
questions either.

October 10

*Joy thrives best in the soil
of thankfulness.*

March 24

I used to have a handle on life,
but then it fell off.

October 9

*P*ray that your "splashes" of
joy will become "showers"
of blessing.

March 25

*W*e're not put on this earth to
see through each other, but to
see each other through.

October 8

Some folks are always complaining;
they put their blues on parade;
but if I wake up in the morning,
I figure I've got it made!

March 26

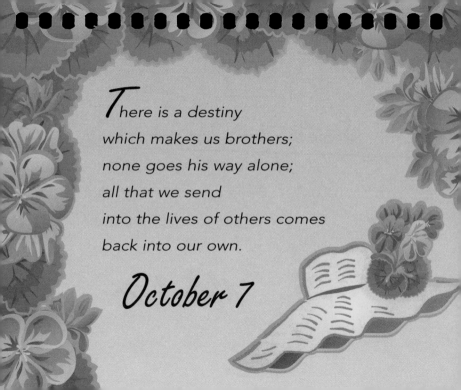

*There is a destiny
which makes us brothers;
none goes his way alone;
all that we send
into the lives of others comes
back into our own.*

October 7

*S*pring is God's way of saying
"One more time!"

March 27

Broken things can become blessed things if you let Christ do the mending.

October 6

A smile is a wrinkle that shouldn't be removed.

March 28

*W*ouldn't it be nice if those
dearest to us were the nearest?

October 5

*W*orry is like a rocking chair: it will give you something to do, but it won't get you anywhere.

March 29

It may be true that life begins at forty, but everything else starts to wear out, fall out, or spread out.

October 4

When you share your joy with others, you double each smile and each laugh; when you share your pain and sorrow, each tear is divided in half.

March 30

*N*ow that we have automatic teller machines, we no longer have to tell our children that money does not grow on trees...they think it comes out of a wall.

October 3

Growing old is mandatory,
growing up is optional.

March 31

*L*ife has a way of coloring your
way of living—but it's you
who chooses the colors.

October 2

I've gone to look for myself.
If I should return before
I get back, keep me here!

April 1

*H*ospitality is making your
guests feel at home even though
you wish they were.

October 1

*S*ome things can be
inherited, but good reputations,
trust, respect, and wages must
all be earned.

April 2

Lord, while You prepare a place for us, prepare us for that place.

September 30

*W*e are Easter people living in
a Good Friday world.

April 3

*N*o matter how great our need, the divine resources are never exhausted.

September 29

I think I need a hug...and a maid and a cook and a chauffeur and a secretary and an accountant...and a lot more hugs.

April 4

A new Chinese diet—eat all
you can, but use only
one chopstick.

September 28

*T*urning to God is always
a right turn.

April 5

*The refiner is never very far
from the mouth of the furnace
when his gold is in the fire.*

September 27

*T*he most important things in
your home are people.

April 6

I love you more than yesterday. Yesterday you really got on my nerves.

September 26

Love cures people—both the ones who give it and the ones who receive it.

April 7

*T*he more you complain,
the longer God lets you live.

September 25

*D*ear God, I have a problem...
it's me.
Dear Child, I have the answer...
it's Me.

April 8

Courage is fighting on, even if you have no plans of how you are going to handle the victory.

September 24

*F*orget the health food.
We need all the preservatives
we can get.

April 9

Nothing is impossible to the people who don't have to do it themselves.

September 23

*T*he right temperature in a home is maintained by warm hearts, not by hot heads.

April 10

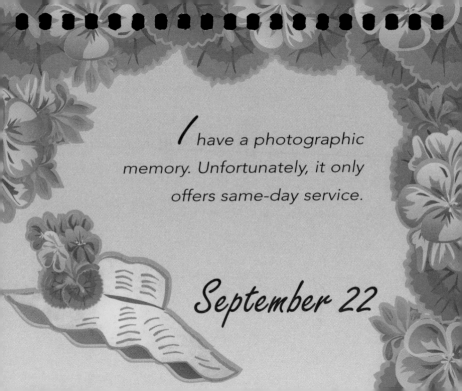

I have a photographic memory. Unfortunately, it only offers same-day service.

September 22

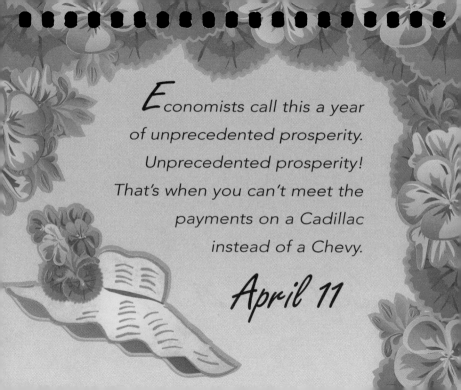

*E*conomists call this a year of unprecedented prosperity. Unprecedented prosperity! That's when you can't meet the payments on a Cadillac instead of a Chevy.

April 11

*A*nxiety does not empty tomorrow of its sorrows, but only empties today of its strength.

September 21

*G*od does not send us answers
to our suffering. Instead, He
takes it upon himself.

April 12

*T*oo many people tell the
same story to the same people
too many times.

September 20

It's hard to be nostalgic when you can't remember anything.

April 13

Worry: The senseless process of using today to clutter up tomorrow's opportunities with leftover problems from yesterday.

September 19

*T*he wind of anger blows out the lamp of intelligence.

April 14

*T*roubles come to pass;
they do not come to stay.

September 18

You cannot do a kindness
too soon, for you never know
how soon it will be too late.

April 15

*W*ithout Jesus we face a hopeless end. But with Jesus we have an endless hope.

September 17

*T*here's only one endeavor in which you can start at the top, and that's digging a hole.

April 16

There will be no crisis next week.
My schedule is already full.

September 16

Life is good for growing things.

April 17

Grandparents are similar to a piece of string—handy to have around and easily wrapped around the fingers of grandchildren.

September 15

Love, like spring rains, is pretty hard to be in the middle of without getting some on you.

April 18

The present is what slips by
us while we're pondering
the past and worrying
about the future.

September 14

*W*e do not remember days,
we remember moments.

April 19

Little Boy's Prayer

Dear God, take care of the whole world. And please, God, take care of yourself, or we're all sunk.

September 13

It's amazing what you can accomplish with a little hard work and a lot of whining.

April 20

*G*od will never lead you where
His grace cannot keep you.

September 12

*S*omewhere over the rainbow—that's where the airline will find my luggage.

April 21

*T*he human tongue is only a few inches away from the brain, but when you listen to some people talk, the two seem miles apart.

September 11

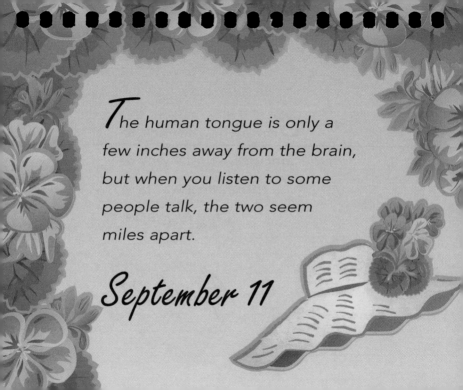

The sound of laughter is God's hand upon a troubled world.

April 22

*L*ife is a constant battle between carrots and chocolate.

September 10

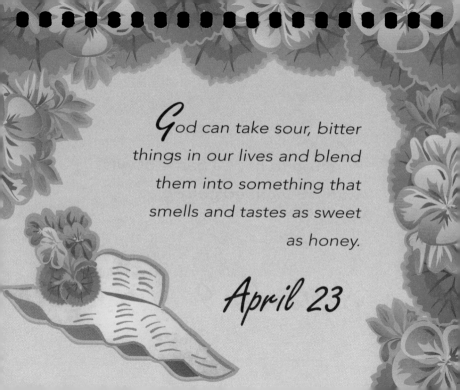

*G*od can take sour, bitter things in our lives and blend them into something that smells and tastes as sweet as honey.

April 23

I refuse to have a battle of wits with an unarmed person.

September 9

*U*se your hindsight to improve your foresight.

April 24

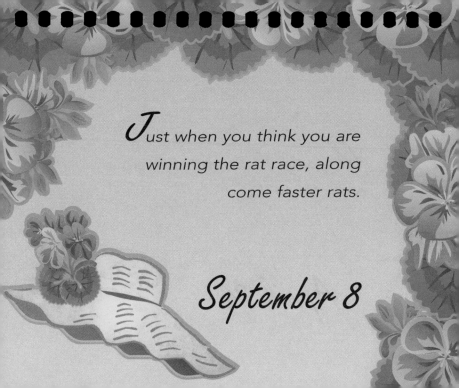

*J*ust when you think you are winning the rat race, along come faster rats.

September 8

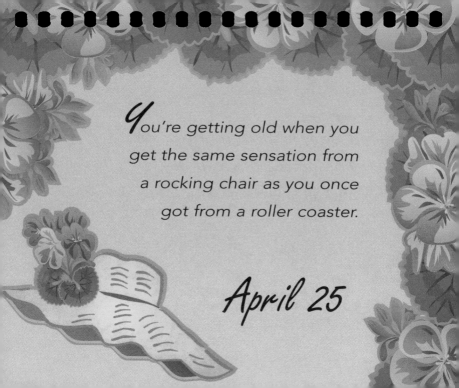

*Y*ou're getting old when you get the same sensation from a rocking chair as you once got from a roller coaster.

April 25

Today is the tomorrow you worried about yesterday, and all is well.

September 7

*F*aith never knows where it is being led, but it loves the One who is leading.

April 26

A penny saved is not
nearly enough.

September 6

You can always return to a friend, like going back to a special place and finding the same warm feeling, untouched by time and distance.

April 27

*A*s you age, what you lose in elasticity, you gain in wisdom...and I think it's a real good trade-off.

September 5

He who laughs last didn't get the joke.

April 28

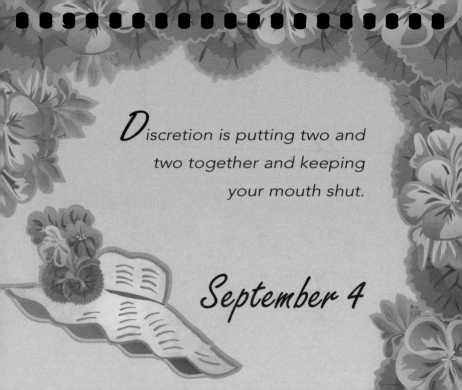

Discretion is putting two and two together and keeping your mouth shut.

September 4

*P*arents: People who bear
infants, bore teenagers,
and board newlyweds.

April 29

It's frustrating when you know all the answers, but nobody bothers to ask you the questions.

September 3

*Perhaps you know why
women over fifty don't
have babies:
They would put them down
somewhere and forget
where they left them.*

April 30

*E*at dessert first!
After all, life is uncertain.

September 2

*M*ay is God's apology
for February.

May 1

My mind not only wanders,
sometimes it leaves
completely.

September 1

I'd unscramble the eggs
if you'd read me the recipe
backwards.

May 2

*T*he rain falls on the just and
the unjust, but chiefly on the just,
because the unjust steals
the just's umbrella.

August 31

If at first you don't succeed,
see if the loser gets anything.

May 3

If I have inside me the stuff to make a cocoon, maybe the stuff of butterflies is there, too.

<small>Trina Paulus</small>

August 30

*M*aking waves almost never
turns the tide.

May 4

*O*ne day I shall burst my buds of calm and blossom into hysteria.

August 29

A lot of kneeling keeps one
in good standing.

May 5

Children can be a great comfort in your old age. And they help you get there faster too.

August 28

Maturity is when we change from cocksureness into thoughtful uncertainty.

May 6

*N*ever lose your head in a battle—you won't have a place to put your helmet.

August 27

*Y*our day goes the way the corners of your mouth turn—
SMILE!

May 7

If you want God's fire to burn brightly in your heart, take out yesterday's ashes.

August 26

If you grasp tomorrow with faith, you know the handle won't fall off.

May 8

*O*ne of life's mysteries is how a two-pound box of candy can make a woman gain five pounds.

August 25

*M*otherhood: If it was going
to be easy, it never would have
started with something
called labor.

May 9

*E*very time I get my act together,
the curtain comes down.

August 24

The most glorious moments in
your life are not the so-called days
of success, but rather, those days
when, out of dejection and despair,
you feel rise within you a challenge
to life and a sense of promise.

May 10

*W*hen dieting remember:
What's on the table eventually
becomes what's on the chair.

August 23

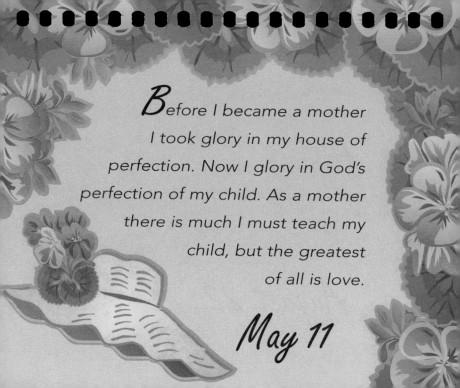

Before I became a mother I took glory in my house of perfection. Now I glory in God's perfection of my child. As a mother there is much I must teach my child, but the greatest of all is love.

May 11

*F*rustration is trying to find your glasses without your glasses.

August 22

You may not be what you
think you are, but what you think,
you are.

May 12

A ship in harbor is safe, but
that is not what ships are for.

August 21

*L*ife isn't always what you
want, but it's what you've got—
so stick a geranium in your hat
and be happy!

May 13

The joy of motherhood: What a woman experiences when all the children are finally in bed.

August 20

*O*n Mother's Day, I think moms should be able to wake up and say to themselves: I'm not just a housewife, I'm a domestic goddess!

May 14

*M*ost people are willing to change, not because they see the light, but because they feel the heat!

August 19

*A*lways take your rainbow
with you!

May 15

There's nothing like a little
experience to upset a theory.

August 18

Things To Do Today:

1. Get up
2. Survive
3. Go to bed

May 16

God made wrinkles to show
where smiles have been.

August 17

A pessimist has no starter,
an optimist has no brakes.

May 17

If ever you make a mistake of judgment, let it be on the side of mercy.

August 16

*M*oms aren't wimps, but they are softies who will do anything for their children.

May 18

*A*n optimist is one who takes
cold water thrown upon his idea,
heats it with enthusiasm, and
uses the steam to push ahead.

August 15

*T*he secret of success is to stay cool and calm on top and paddle like crazy underneath.

May 19

*Y*ou cannot buy enthusiasm, loyalty, or the devotion of hearts, minds, or souls. You must earn these.

August 14

If you can remain calm, you just don't have all the facts.

May 20

Age is a high price to pay
for maturity.

August 13

'*T* is better to have loved and
lost...much better.

May 21

A good listener is not only popular everywhere, but after a while he knows something.

August 12

Stress Reducer: Put a bag on your head. Mark it "Closed for Remodeling."

May 22

True repentance has a double aspect—it looks upon things past with a weeping eye and upon the future with a watchful eye.

August 11

*W*e don't have to be happy to laugh. Indeed, we become happy because we laugh.

May 23

*L*ost:
Dog with three legs, blind in left eye, missing right ear, tail broken, and recently castrated. Answers to the name of "Lucky."

August 10

Do more than exist...Live!
Do more than touch...Feel!
Do more than look...See!
Do more than hear...Listen!
Do more than talk...
Say something!

May 24

Any child can tell you that the sole purpose of a middle name is so he can tell when he's really in trouble.

August 9

Childhood is like the old joke about a small town—one blink and it's gone.

May 25

I'm not rich and famous, but I do have priceless grandchildren.

August 8

*H*appiness is not a station you arrive at, but a manner of traveling.

May 26

*Thank goodness for August—
the time to lie back and wallow
in the knowledge that there is
absolutely no occasion
to rise to.*

August 7

*G*od promises us daily bread—
not flour for a year in advance.

May 27

You can't please everybody
no matter what you do.

August 6

There was an old lady
  named Myrtle
who bought herself a new girdle.
She held in her breath,
it squeezed her to death.
Now the graveyard is
  fertile with Myrtle.

May 28

Maturity begins when we're content to feel we're right about something without feeling the necessity to prove someone else wrong.

August 5

*S*orrow looks back,
worry looks around,
faith looks up.

May 29

*T*here's no such thing as improvement without work.

August 4

A girl joining an exercise class was told to wear loose clothing. She said, "If I had any loose clothing, I wouldn't be joining the class."

May 30

*L*anguage is the apparel in which our thoughts parade before the public. Never clothe them in vulgar or shoddy attire.

August 3

Some carve out the future;
others just whittle.

May 31

God put me on earth to accomplish a certain number of things. Right now I am so far behind, I will never die.

August 2

*T*ake time to laugh—it is
the music of the soul.

June 1

*M*osquitoes are like small children. The minute they stop making noise you know they are into something.

August 1

The pessimist complains about the wind, the optimist expects it to change, and the realist adjusts the sails.

June 2

*Y*ou've reached middle age
when all you exercise is caution.

July 31

I finally got my head together,
and my body fell apart.

June 3

Tourist: A person who travels a thousand miles to get a picture of himself standing by his car.

July 30

*A*s you get older it's best to do things when you think of them...or you'll forget.

June 4

Good sense is easier to have than use.

July 29

*T*he Lord gave us two ends—
one to sit on and the other to
think with. Success depends on
which one we use the most.

June 5

*F*riendship multiplies joy
and divides grief.

July 28

I know things are tough right now, but just remember, every flower that ever bloomed had to go through a whole lot of dirt to get there!

June 6

*E*very time I think about
exercise, I lie down 'til the
thought goes away.

July 27

*E*at a live toad first thing in the morning, and nothing worse can happen to you the rest of the day!

June 7

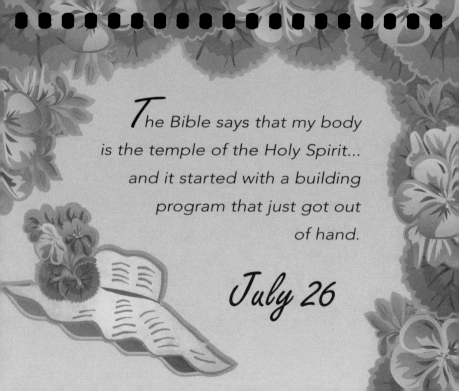

*T*he Bible says that my body
is the temple of the Holy Spirit...
and it started with a building
program that just got out
of hand.

July 26

*T*hose to whom I can't relate
I'm proud to say are very few;
But I wonder why it is that they
Are people I'm related to.

June 8

*B*eing different isn't the same as making a difference.

July 25

*T*he only way to look younger
is to not be born so soon.

June 9

Life is easier than you think—all you have to do is this: accept the impossible, do without the indispensable, bear the intolerable, and be able to smile at anything.

July 24

*Y*outh: By the time your face
clears up, your mind gets fuzzy.

June 10

What we need is more milk of human kindness in the cream of society.

July 23

*Y*ou know you're getting old when you stoop to tie your shoes and wonder what else you can do while you're down there.

June 11

*T*he reward for work well done
is the opportunity to do more.

July 22

*D*on't let the best you have
done so far be the standard
for the rest of your life.

June 12

*S*ome days you're the bug;
some days, the windshield!

July 21

*T*ime may be a great healer...
but it's a lousy beautician.

June 13

*S*uccess consists of getting
up just one more time than
you've fallen down.

July 20

*W*hen it's all said and done, when all the opinions have been uttered, preached, shouted, and shared, there is only one thing we can do: From this moment on...love.

June 14

A handful of patience is worth
more than a bushel of brains.

July 19

*A*venge yourself: Live long
enough to be a problem
to your children.

June 15

*Yesterday is experience,
tomorrow is hope...
today is getting from
one to the other.*

July 18

You don't stop laughing because you grow old...you grow old because you stop laughing.

June 16

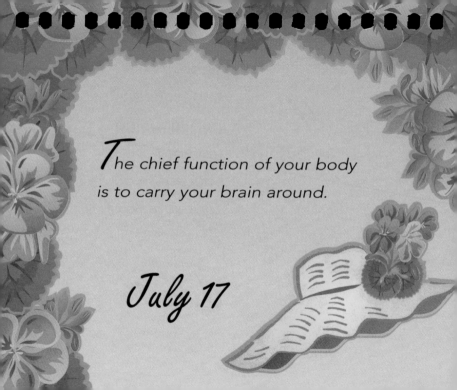

*T*he chief function of your body
is to carry your brain around.

July 17

Sign on a fish market in Anaheim: Our fish are so fresh you wanna smack 'em.

June 17

Adolescence is the awkward age when a child is too old to say something cute and too young to say something sensible.

July 16

A diet is something that you keep putting off while you keep putting on.

June 18

*N*oah didn't wait for his ship to come in...he built one!

July 15

The most efficient water power
in the world is a child's tears.

June 19

*O*ne nice thing about growing older is that you and your children eventually wind up on the same side of the generation gap.

July 14

*H*umor is the hole that lets the
sawdust out of a stuffed shirt.

June 20

*T*ruth does not depend on
a consensus of opinion.

July 13

*M*y memory is excellent. There are only three things I can't remember. I can't remember faces, I can't remember names, and...I've forgotten the third thing.

June 21

Ideas are like children—no matter how much you admire someone else's, you can't help liking your own best.

July 12

*T*he best way to forget all
your troubles is to wear
tight shoes.

June 22

*P*eople who say nothing is impossible should try gargling with their mouths closed.

July 11

*L*ife not only begins at forty—
it begins to show.

June 23

*A*ge is like love...
it cannot be hidden.

July 10

*S*ince I've been backing into middle age, I don't have any idea where I'm going.

June 24

*W*hat light? I'm still looking for the tunnel!

July 9

*T*he people who tell you
never to let little things worry you
have never tried sleeping in the
same room with a mosquito.

June 25

*W*e must accept finite disappointment, but we must never lose infinite hope.

July 8

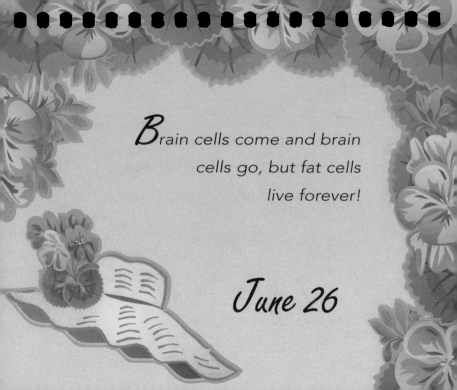

*B*rain cells come and brain
cells go, but fat cells
live forever!

June 26

*T*ake a tip from nature:
Your ears aren't made to shut,
but your mouth is.

July 7

*S*ome people grow up and spread cheer...others just grow up and spread.

June 27

Our aim in life improves as we grow older, but it seems that we soon run out of ammunition.

July 6

*L*ife's golden age is when
the kids are too old to need
baby-sitters and too young
to borrow the family car.

June 28

A bore is a fellow who persists in talking about himself when you want to talk about yourself.

July 5

A grudge is too heavy a load for anyone to carry.

June 29

Your final exit will be your
greatest entrance.

July 4

The best exercise for good
relationships is bending
over backward.

June 30

Every family tree has
a little sap.

July 3

Don't miss the beautiful colors of the rainbow while you're looking for the pot of gold at the end of it.

July 1

*T*he nice part of living in
a small town is that when
I don't know what I'm doing,
someone else does.

July 2